My Life,
My World,
My Truth

Poems by Jason A. Grant

authorHOUSE®

AuthorHouse™
1663 Liberty Drive
Bloomington, IN 47403
www.authorhouse.com
Phone: 1-800-839-8640

First published by AuthorHouse   7/20/2010

ISBN: 978-1-4520-4752-2 (sc)

Library of Congress Control Number: 2010910033

Printed in the United States of America
Bloomington, Indiana

This book is printed on acid-free paper.

For those who have come before us, those who will come after us and for all brave enough to be a little different.

Contents

I
Butterscotch & Now-and-Laters

We the Poets

We the poets of this world
Declare our power to use words as bombs
And we Black and Brown poets...
We *original* poets, with our words
That vibrate through the air like drums
Have always been on the frontlines
Of all battles
Fearlessly dreaming through debris of disdain
Overcoming attempted thefts of our voices, rhythms, and ideas
We are here now
We *original* poets have been here from the beginning
Framing the glory of our kinfolk
In meticulous Nubian carved metaphors
While being forced to swallow poisons to our soul
Resistant to the toxins, we rose to defy expectations
Persistent in our stance, we built castles out of dirt and sand
Using love as our canvas...
Strength as our paint brush...
We have created a masterpiece called "struggle"
And from this masterpiece we have reached the pinnacle of human beauty
Priceless is our story that we tell
Let all generations study our odyssey
In pursuit of a greater potential reality
We the poets declare our capacity to use our minds as instruments...
Instruments for rebellion
And we *original* poets, in the making of a new day,
We assert our freedom to be...
To be molded in our own language
Without consideration of the feelings of those who desire our decline
In these words, we define the greatness of our reflections
This is us...
We are real...
We will pass it on.

Sun Journal

I saw the sun this morning for the first time in four days. It felt good… It felt good to my skin and it felt good to squint my eyes to alleviate the sun's shine. It felt good to see the sky light up; it felt good to see the clouds clear out, and it felt good to see the "blue heavens."

I saw the sun this morning for the first time in four days. I was glad… I was glad that I awoke today. I was glad to look out of the window and see the sunlight reflect off of the windshields of the cars outside. I was glad to hear the birds chirping in excitement over a warm summer day. I was glad that I walked the few blocks to work after getting out of the subway. I was glad to see the children waiting to "erupt" in play, as only children can. And I was glad that I could smile again.

I saw the sun this morning for the first time in four days. Maybe that was the reason why… Maybe that was the reason why I felt "like a kid again" today. Maybe that was the reason why that little girl helped me open the mailbox this morning – the sun must've made her feel good too. Maybe that was the reason why this ghetto looked like Park Avenue to me this morning. Maybe that was the reason why home doesn't seem so far away. Maybe that was the reason why I felt like I could cry today.

Jayku (Ode to the Dance)

Let the music
Take you
Beyond the usual cares
And concerns of life
Let the rhythm
Move your hips
To a synchrony
That leaves the
Rhythm-less envious
Let the sound
Hold you
In a way
That makes
The righteous
Believe that
Your every twist
And turn is a
Sign of savage
And uncivilized sin
Let the music,
Rhythms
And sound
Of the drums
Free you.

I Am Africa (I Am the Motherland)

I am...
I am the mother...
I am the mother of existence...
Of Civilization
My children are kissed by the sun...
Caressed by beauty
Yet many of my children fail to acknowledge me
I am Africa
I am the motherland
I was the mother even when I was...
Named something else...
Before someone decided to call me Africa
My children are spread all over the world
And they crossed oceans before anyone else ever crossed them
Explored valleys before anyone else ever explored them
Created what no one else could ever create
But my children were never rewarded
Many of my children were ripped away from me
Locked, chained, sold, tortured, raped, and executed...
For profit.
Robbed, massacred, exploited, exiled, imprisoned, and disenfranchised...
For the sake of "manifest destiny"
Some of my children even helped in the terror
And they don't remember...
They can't.
My children have been conditioned to forget...
Taught to vilify me
Many of those who have been reminded, don't want to remember
But I am still The Mother.
The Olmecs (Ulmecs), the Mayans, the Aztecs, the Incas, Teotihuacán,
Yoruba, Ibo (Igbo), Bantu, Bambara, Berber, Nilotes, "the Aborigines"
(My children)
Haiti to Mali, and Nigeria to New York, and Grenada to Ghana
From South Carolina to South Africa
From Cuba to the Congo
Mexico to Mozambique, California to Cameroon,
Massachusetts to Madagascar, Libya to Louisiana,

Brazil to Botswana
Puerto Rico and Dominican Republic to Ethiopia and Sierra Leone,
Jamaica to Kenya
From D.C. to Guinea,
Tunisia to Tennessee, Belize to Benin,
Ecuador to Egypt... Yes, Egypt, too.
I am the Mother, the Father, and the Children.
I am the roots of humanity.
I AM AFRICA!

Haiku

Conformity is
More than shackles on the soul
Are we to be free?

Poems by Jason A. Grant

Follicle

I have a wooly crown
Growing from the pours within the skin
On my skull
Every follicle representing
Long histories and her-stories
Of Nubians long past
Reflecting societal and scientific formulas
On pyramidal walls
My "hair"
As you call it
Untamable by even the most iron shears
That with which Samson wishes he could bring back
But I retain the power innate to my own
Natural to the lion as marrow to the bone
I stand loud with the kinks glowing with the sun
Alive and well even in the valleys of repulsion
Firm is each strand...
Firm is each strand crinkling in the humidity of an August heat wave
I reject conformist calls for its obliteration
My contention is that the sign will arrive
When it is time to part ways
And place this crown
On memorial ground
As I see fit to render it
My vigorous mane
Abundant in your rebelliousness
Live.

Haiku

Black hair... strong like the
Ties that bind me to brilliant
Nations; live through me.

NGBA (No Good Brothas Available)

This topic has been repeated more times that I would like to count
Beating the same old drum
I'm almost weary of getting up on this soapbox mount
To counterbalance the misrepresentation
That is so often the main idea of a sisterly conversation –
"Where have all the good brothas gone?"
And it's the same old song of the brown swan
Complaining of men who can't keep up with their lofty standards -
Jobless, ugly, uneducated, lazy and no manners
The "good brothas" are taken, gay or hooked on white women
And with the personification of the "down low" identified with Black men,
What's a sistah to do?
So she's looking in my direction, saying, "oh no, not you!"
But no, no, excuse me
But I know I'm just not the one; walking around performing poetry for free
The poet-at-large gets no love from his presence on the mic
Too much mileage on his legs indicates no car, not even a bike
Because good brothas don't use public transportation
But I can't say that I'm one to change that inclination
I'm no longer interested in proving assumptions wrong
I've gone too long being indifferent to the rationalizing of the superficial
And working two jobs leaves no time to correct what's not official
I will not be left wondering "what was wrong with me?"
Maybe it was everything except the partridge in a pear tree
Or maybe I wasn't too interested in showing off my credentials again
Because, instead of being framed on my walls, the college degree, law degree and bar certificate are still in the envelopes they came in
And frankly who's to say that the strength of your *résumé* determines whether you're a good man or not
Straight from the block, my diploma from the school of hard-knocks is my treasured rock
Believe it if you will, men are thinking about similar things

But we don't have to worry about waiting for a mate who can give us "the ring."
So, in your journey to find that "good brotha" to provide for ya'
Look deep before you leap into the arms of any ol' lover
There are some good brothas available
Maybe not a lot
If you can't find one, don't worry... you may want to pick a white guy out of the pot.

Haiku

Who told you I like
Fish, shrimp, crab or lobster tail?
I'd rather eat grass.

I am Going to Fly Today

I... am... going... to... fly... today!
I am going to fly today because walking on land no longer satisfies me;
Nor does it fulfill my necessary travels.
I would say that I'm going to walk on water, but I don't want to be accused of being blasphemous today.
Deciding to shy away slightly from my usual controversy creations,
I'm going to do something much more outlandish... to you... I'm going to fly!
I'm going to fly... in the air... high like Ben Franklin's kite.
I won't be "on anything" besides the clouds in the highest of elevations.
And I won't have to worry about airport security
I won't have to worry about metal detectors and random searches
I won't have to take off my shoes so they may be checked for shoe-bombs.
I am just going to lift off on my own.
Oh, and no wings, I don't want feathers shedding all over the place.
I am just going to fly high in the air like the big metal airplanes that amazed people decades ago... up in the sky in all its glory. I am going to fly like that big white dog thing in the "Never-ending Story"... y'all remember that?
Because gravity has become increasingly burdensome, and I just want to touch the clouds just one time.
I want to touch the clouds just one time to find out if they really taste like candy or have any taste at all.
And even more remarkable than a man flying in the air who is not a character from your favorite comic book, is the fact that I really don't care who says it's impossible.
I don't care about the probable odds against me.
I want to be free in my defiance of the laws of science.
Free of these restraints, I will expect to resist any usual expectations of normalcy... of the ordinary... of conventional humanity.
I will fly....

Word Life

It's only a word
Words can't hurt you
Words have no power
Words are just that – words.
If words have no power, no one would care about Shakespeare or Giovanni
No one would care about Angelou or Baraka
Frost or Fitzgerald
Who would need a Richard Wright or James Baldwin?
Sonia Sanchez or Langston Hughes...
Zora Neale or Gwendolyn Brooks
Because poets would be unnecessary
And poems couldn't be used as weapons to the armless
And songs would not be used as soundtracks to rebellion
No one would sit down and listen to a song and say,
"I can *feel* that"
I can feel Billie Holiday and Bessie Smith
I can feel Marvin and Stevie and Smokey
And Aretha and Ella...
Sing about highs and lows of love and life
But no one would *feel* that because words are just that – words
But words have life and feeling, and the feeling of love doesn't come from
your words, brother.
How you gonna say that? You know I got love for you, nigga...
I love you so much, I call you *my nigga.*
Love, Black man? Love?
Then give love, Black man
Love me like your brother
Your blood
Your twin
Your son
Your cousin
Your nephew
Your heart
Your friend
Show me that love you speak of
That love, that great love my brother has for his brother.
Love, Black man, love!
Understand it and breathe life into it.

The Truth

The truth is... I don't know what the truth is / flames are alive / and every time a child cries, tears are really falling from God's eyes / Engaging in consumptions of emptiness / and, and, and soliloquies trump serenades / while minds wander in wonderfully wasted waves of wishes / Is it unrealistic to dream in peace about peace? / Take the blood from my arms & take the pride from my eyes / In depths of my thoughts are fears of loneliness / Fears of losing the way to the truth / Fears of never finding the truth / and truthfully, the truth keeps escaping me and returning as something newly... unexpected / Glory is hard to find in a world full of loss / Searching becomes a difficult game in itself / and after every hill there is another hole to fall in / The truth, or as close to the truth as I know, is powerful / strong and benevolent / liberating / euphoric / yet they say the truth hurts... a lot - A finger digging into a knife wound; all of your toenails being ripped off one by one, a bone completely shattered – That's what the truth is supposed to feel like / Live with the pain of the truth or the pain of the unknown – doesn't seem like much of a choice / seek truths or deny the existence of fallacies – maybe that's the decision / But the truth is, I don't know what the truth is / And that is the only truth I do know.

Harm/Harmless

If you look at my life, you'll see complex images
Far from simplistic
Ideas ranging from naïve to pessimistic
I stand alone – free / I am – loneliness – imprisoned… in these walls /
separated
No giggling allowed / the seriousness of the situation compels me
To be tactfully detached from peace / peace of mind / would you like a
piece…
Of my pie / with a slice of bologna on a slice of rye / hopes and dreams are
just those – hopes and dreams… with hopelessness not far behind / just /
wait…ing / to / con…sume / you…
With constant con/tra/dic/tions and pseudo-emotional manumissions
I am deteriorating in front of my eyes, but there's no harm.
Harmless
Mind-warped from mine own work
("Don't ask me again. Don't ask me again.")
Authorize my de---pressed eyes / de---sensitize me from grieving eyes –
cries
And cries
And cry
I cry, because that's all I know how to do right… right now
Dwindling down a path, trying to capture the uncatchable or the already
captured
Self-muti-la---tion on my part for unfulfilled empty heart
Full loving strong heart
Unloved hard heart… stone heart
Harmlessness
I am trembling in repeated repulsions / pulsating reactions to casual
interactions
Causal as-a-matter-of-fact-tions / attractions / delirium from imitations
Unsuccessful adjustments and acclamations to environmental
complications
And variations – it's all I can stand
There are no "if's", "but's", "and's"
With this harmful harmless harmlessness.

Haiku

The silence is so
Blindingly loud that I have
Been deafened to tears.

I Want to Cry Today

I want to cry today.
No reason... I just feel that I need a good cry. Any kind of cry, it doesn't matter. It could be an ugly-face cry, a one-tear cry, anything.
Something to keep me from going crazy.
Something that will tell me that I'm still human and not some emotionless bulk of skin and bones.
Why is that so difficult?
Why does it take so much to get it out?
I just want to cry.
Seems simple enough, but it isn't.
I'm feeling lost in this world.
Lost in the senselessness all around me; all around my life.
The steps I take are muttered by these "things" – these inconsequential happenings just hamper any attempt at happiness.
So you would think the tears would start flowing, but NOOOOO!
The tears are just being difficult to spite me.
Maybe there's nothing really to cry over.
I guess I've just become desensitized to all of this mess.
Now I have to deal with it.
I guess there is no way around it, huh?
I just have to make peace with... oh, no, wait, I was wrong. Here it comes....

Why?

This hard week comes with as many frustrations as usual.
I have no idea how to heal this.
I'm not sure how to recover from the intrinsic nature of frustration and intimate complexities that always seem to get on my nerves. I'm tired.
I don't know why I have these issues that make my head hurt at least 10 times a month.
I know in some way, I do have control over these powered annoyances, because I allow this stuff to happen. I allow myself to tolerate the bull...
I am forever allowing myself to tolerate the bull that results from the failures of expectations of the people around me. And I don't know if they disappoint me or if I disappoint myself.
So now, I'm sitting here on a cold damp winter night sitting with a pen and a pad trying to clear my mind on the paper. I feel like I'm on a lonely beach, feeling the coarse sand get stuck between my toes. I'm looking out over the waters, seeing the sun go down behind the waves – hypnotized.
Looking at the glow of the sky, asking the question "why?"

Isn't it strange?

Isn't it strange?

        Life is so precious, but people take it for granted.

Isn't it strange that the supposedly best times in your life can be the toughest?
Isn't it strange?

        That older people always want
        Children to act like adults
        But still treat them like babies...
        They want you to be responsible
        But still have the nerve
        To make decisions for you
Isn't it strange that the phrase "keepin' it real" is overused by people who are as fake as Payless Shoes?
And it is so strange how love can start so beautifully and yet can end so painfully...

        ... that people who you thought were
        Your friends are always
        "Gone with the Wind."
And isn't it strange that I've seen so much in my life at such a young age?

Haiku

Seemingly free from
Regret you pause in the spot-
Light of freedom's pulse.

Haiku

Imposter smiles hide
Alias melancholy
Through spirit, I awake.

The Tragic Negro

Mister or Ms. Tragic Negro
Conditioned to heal by mental placebo
Everything Caucasian you worship and idol
You hope it rubs off, but it nuh guh suh!

Trapped by the conventional thoughts and beliefs
Yet ignore the truth in what you sow, you reap
Suffering miserably, you nag and complain
Yet contribute to the madness, no progress is gained
Now it's evident in your primp and pose
Unease with your reflection, so persist in pinching your nose
Chemically alter every follicle of hair
Born as mahogany, now bleached to fair
Boast of diamonds, cars and jewels
Bend over forward to play the fool
Now you play conscious, new Kente, new 'fro
Read a little Huey & Bobby, now you the Black pro?
Impress your peers with 4 or 5 words in Swahili
Yet continue to be caged by your "if it ain't white, it ain't right"
mentality
Now you're a lost child, evading the truth
Beauty lacerations to salvage your youth
Desperately hoping everyone is fooled by your disguise
"My tragic Negro-ness, they'll never surmise"
With all the precautions you thought you took
Never thought you'd be found out in only one look
Dysfunction in purpose, identity, love, and the cause of self-strife
The Tragic Negro, another imitation of life.

Haiku

    Part 1
Imitation of
Manhood; displayed through sagging
Jeans and crotch-grab fits.
    Part 2
Making the mental
Fall to brown "lost boys" stuck in
Ghetto Neverlands.

Moody Artist Rains

The Moody Artist Rains pour down like the skies opened up with no limits. There's a flood. There are no clear ways to walk; you're stuck in mud waist-high and the roots of the trees have been uncovered like the pain of the heart. It's that hard drag of the blues, tempered with the usual obstacles, downfalls and tragedies of life. Yeah, that's it...

Normalcy is confusing to the artist – is it a good thing? Is it a bad thing? He doesn't know. He cries by himself in the sunlight, unashamed of the clouds that will come by night. The moonlight is ever more obstructed by the coming waters. Is this going to be the big one?

Maybe.

But who is there for the artist? Whose shoulder does the artist cry on to spare all others around him of the inclement emotional thunderstorm?

He.

Is.

In.

One.

Of.

His.

Moods.

Again...

The ups are limited and the downs are dominant in this story... after it's all done, apologies are necessary, but not easily forthcoming. Not because "sorry" is hard to say, but it's hard to hear when everyone is gone.

Swept away.

The artist dreams in daylight again, no longer moody, but taken aback by the ear-numbing silence that blows in his direction. He searches. He fantasizes about the mending of bridges. He rests, and he hopes to find survivors.

Haiku

The rhythms shake the
Walls; I can see the paint dance
Off into the cracks.

They Never Told Me...

They never told me that "Black is beautiful"
Maybe if I lived in the sixties and seventies with a glowing afro and finely knitted dashikis, I would have loved myself more
Instead, I was born in the eighties, when Geri-curls were the thing to do
Grew up in the nineties when the sistas loved extensions, weaves and perms of all kinds...
Light skin was "in," narrow noses were cute, and everyone wanted hazel, green or blue eyes – real, fake or otherwise
Maybe because they never told us...
And they never told me....
They never told me that this brown skin is the envy of folks aplenty
They never told me that these full lips were to be worshipped, not be ashamed of
They never told me that this kinky hair on my head would be a treasure others can only dream of
Maybe it's good that they never told me
Because now I will never let them forget.

Hazy Moon

Hazy moon
How'd you get there?
Did I fall too soon?
Hazy moon, high in the sky
Our light fills the room
Hazy moon, how'd you get those eyes, ba-by?
Let my mind consume.

Anniversary (9/11... '02)

You ever wake up with a heavy feeling?
Just got outta' bed, and can't move...
That's today?
That's today...
A little girl got on the bus
Her school uniform nicely ironed and simply styled: white shirt and navy blue skirt
She looked at her transfer ticket and said,
"Oooh, September the eleventh"
It seems to be a real quiet morning
Not unusually quiet, not usually quiet, just... quiet
Like it's / just / one / of / those/ days/
Just / another / one / of / those... no... no
The people on the train are silent
Isn't this D.C.? – The District of Commotion?
Brother on my right with the sniffles breaks up the lull
Mmmph, mmmph, mmmph
Mmmph, mmmph, mmmph
 It must be contagious
Mmmph, mmmph
He's listening to his portable CD player
To break the monotony, I presume
Blown noses
Then silence
No conversations
(Train operator: "Next stop, L'Enfant Plaza, doors opening on the left")
Folks came in, but must have left their tongues outside
Because there were no voices
Just more silence
Only the train had the audacity to scream and screech
I saw a guy with an American flag sticking out of his pocket
Is that what today's about?
All patriots day?
Hmmm...
It's 8:46am
Saw an unnecessarily large American flag
It was being held up by the Metro maintenance guy

It's 9:37am
Ding-dong, ding-dong, ding-dong
More silence
It seems like a real quiet morning will become a real quiet day
Not unusually quiet, not usually quiet, just quiet
Like it's / just / one / of / those / days /
Just / another / one / of / those... no... no...
Not today....

Playas, Pimps, and Posers

What up, pimp?
What up, playa?
See, in this game of life...
You have your playas...
Your pimps...
And your posers...
But really, they're all the same
Dig it, brothas and sistas...
Pimps pimp to make money off of others
Playas play to make enamored fools out of the unsuspecting
But they all pose like they have power...
When all they have is temporary...
Temporary money
Temporary booty
Temporary influence
They pose strength...
But without their victims, they're weak
To eliminate their weakness, they reproduce others...
Others to follow in their poser footsteps
You can see them all over
Don't fall for the typical image of fur coats...
Shiny snakeskin shoes...
And "pimp hats"
Playas and pimps pose in "wife-beaters"...
Blue jeans...
Air Jordan's...
And doo-rags
Grabbin' their nuts to hold up their lack of manhood
Celebrating themselves on street corners and boardrooms...
Red carpets and project hallways...
Laughing all the way to the poser hall of fame.

It's a Black Woman's World

My sisters!
Queens!
Astounding perseverance through journeys across nations, across hemispheres... with heads held as high as possible, even with so much of the world on your shoulders.
Press on.
Wear your crowns and shed your chains; take your place in the sun.
The strength you possess cannot be compared to any other:
Woman
Leader
Sister
Wife
Queen
Mother
I stand by you, fight along side of you, live with you, and love because of you, with the hope that you'll see why you should be cherished.
Wear your crowns and shed your chains; take your place in the sun.
We have taken you for granted for too long... let it end today.
You have been attacked for being too strong... let it end today.
Let your soul and mind guide the peace you want to find.
This is your world; we're just inhabitants waiting for your every word, adjusting to your every movement.
Your world can be filled with peace and love, with no more wars and battles on the horizon.
Wear your crowns and shed your chains; take your place in the sun.

Nothing Nothings

Conflict and horror the world over
See blue skies turn into napalm gray
Charred flesh raining from the clouds
There is *nothing* left
Nothing.
Peace is a memory while bombs fly religiously
What is lacking is an auspice of faith in the shadows of spiritual warfare
But decades-old battles have not come to a respite
Despite all the rhetoric of diplomacy, we can't seem to break these...
Nothing nothings
Booming voices dissecting spirits
Parsing belief into segments of ownership of a grand spirit
We believe in the segments more than anything
It keeps us feeling special
But it is really more nothings
Nothing
Rising above, I meditate like Buddha in eastern valleys
Deflecting judgmental stones with JE-SUS
I greet you with peace
Salaam
And unto you peace
Salaam
Let your spirit be free
Salaam
Dance to the sound of the wind
Salaam
Grace us with your light
Salaam
     Peace
       Love.

I Can Fly Higher Now

I looked at my neighbor in a different light the other day
I saw her eyes as a beautiful ocean of white with a center of dark brown
glaze
Within those eyes was a story of a people
A people unknown to me, a people I had not the experience from which
to see.
A story barely spoken of
A story misrepresented as having no spirit, civilization or love.
Many a day, these eyes go unnoticed
A secondary concern, for which many care not to solace.
Quiet is the gloom which **HIS**tory has placed on this soul
Deafening is the effect of hundreds of years of theft and tear-causing
massacres still untold.
So I started to search
To search for that part of me that could see life through her vision
That part of me that could hear and let in the voices of a past that
history books never gave admission.
And now, I can fly
I can fly because the wings of understanding have grown from my mind
I can fly because I have traveled over the barriers that the cynical say
can only be imagined to find.
And I saw pain where, with the naked eye, there was none
I heard happiness and laughter with no mouths to come from.
I saw the tears that filled oceans and smiles that brightened the sky
I heard the answers to the many questions of who, what where and
why.
And now I am able to put my wings around her, because I have found
what was hidden behind those eyes and within that heart
And our different shades of brown are combined, when some would
want them apart.
No longer are our struggles separated
Our hearts and minds with understanding are completely filled
And I can fly higher now, and **WE** can fly higher still.

On Gorgeous Day

On this gorgeous day, the sun is shining...
Beyond its normal glow
The wind moves ever so calmly...
As to touch the skin with just a whisper of its power
Cumulous clouds giving 2 minutes of welcomed shade...
As the waters of the pond ripple with small waves...
Forcing the comfortable geese to fly off their convenient floating spot.

On gorgeous day, the trees look extra beautiful
The squirrels climb the young and old trees with a little extra pep in their
step
Throwing small pieces of tree limb and acorns around...
In a lively game of nature catch.
On this gorgeous day, the children run and jump with unfettered glee
Rightfully nervous parents scream for their children to stay close
But their exuberant youthfulness is hypnotized by nature's beauty
Calling them to disobey their parents...
And behave with the utmost rebellion.
On this gorgeous day, this absolutely stunning day,
I am reminded that we humans really compromise the greatness of our
planet's majesty
Forcing it to turn on itself
Oh, on gorgeous day, how I wonder if we can preserve this splendor.

Butterscotch & Now-and-Laters

Butterscotch and Now-and-Laters for 25 cents at the corner candy store!
Six years old without a care in the world
Planning our strategy in freeze-tag
Because we were too cool for dodge-ball
And too fly for hide-and-seek
Our claim to fame was being masters of the open fire hydrant
Champions of "Connect Four"
This was our little world...
Our little universe...
Of handball and "suicide"
While the big kids played "craps" and blackjack
We survived on "Uno" and "I declare war"
Three o'clock meant more than the end of the school day
It signified the afternoon main event
"Which heavyweight bully would challenge the unsuspecting lightweight nerd in the battle for elementary school supremacy?!!!"
Butterscotch and Now-and-Laters were our candy of choice
Jolly ranchers and jawbreakers not too far behind
As we sat, reciting the words to "Beat it" and "Billie Jean"
Moonwalking on concrete
Spinning on the pavement
Watching the big kids play football in between traffic and parked cars
While we took turns trying to outrun every car that sped down the block
Waiting for the unforgettable tune of the Mister Softee Ice Cream truck to pass through
Begging our less than pleased parents for one dollar to buy an ice cream cone
I never liked sprinkles, but most kids did...
Not too far behind Mister Softee was the Italian Ices man
Just in case you couldn't get the dollar from your mom fast enough to catch Mister Softee, the Italian Ices man was there to fulfill your craving
This was our world...
Watching it all from the front of our six floor apartment building...
Or the better view from our third floor fire escape...
Six years old without a care in the world...
This was our universe...

We didn't have pool parties at the neighbors
We had block parties and "party at Janet's crib"
While the latest hot records blasted from Tony's boombox...
Or from every other car that rolled through the avenue...
And all we could do is smile and laugh
Because... we had it all.

II

Scorpio:
Love Poems and Not-So-Ordinary Love
Poems

Ode to the Sister I Saw on the Train Last Week

Now how do I do this right? What really are the right words to speak?
They gotta be smooth, gotta be tight; anything less, you`ll say my game
was weak.
The sister I saw on the train last week.
Almond eyes lady, bronze skin woman, "Ms. Ivory Smile."
You sure do know how to fill those jeans to the farthest mile.
Saw the look on your face when I stepped up,
"Not another guy who just wants to f@*k."
Not to offend, but I don`t think I can be compared to your former men.
A little bit different, as you can contend.
I was just feeling the way you walked through those sliding doors.
All eyes were on you, like you appeared through the floor.
Can`t believe I had this opportunity to lay my eyes on you.
Not even dreams can be this cruel.
So you must be real.
Now I hope I can close the deal.
"Excuse me, how you doin`? I saw you over here and I knew I had to say
something.
My name is...."

Soul Mate

You know how the saying goes
"Something old, something new…"
But how about **something beautiful, something real…**
Yeah…
Yeah, it's you.
I just wanted to share something with you;
It's nothing flashy, or extravagant, or expensive…
It's just… the rest of my life.
I know doing this won't be easy since I've never had a lot to give anyone,
but I can give you… my heart and the soul that you inspired.
My mind… The same mind that your mind has made love to numerous
times.
I see my future in your eyes; my happiness in your smile.
If you would allow me…
I'd like to face the world with you.

Beautiful One: a goodbye letter

Dear Beautiful One,
With piercing eyes of inquisitive intensity
Have mercy on my spirit
I am at a lost for words to describe missing all that is you
I have come to know the pace of your mind
And I am always astonished how your voice breathes oxygen into my
lungs
But I know now that it is not meant for me
I wish I could give up everything...
To love you just one full day
To hold you until the sun rises over your face
I could beg you... to stay,
As much as I thirst for the water conceived from your touch,
But the best way to allow you to love is to let you go
Boundless goddess
You have exceeded my capacity to wonder
But like being stranded on a deserted island,
You are your own greatest companion and cohort
An enigma all to yourself
The greatest mystery is...
Who am I to think that you could come down from your star long
enough to live and love without the question of creation and all that is
existence dancing firmly in your head?
While everyone but a few inquire about your sanity
I am comforted by my inarticulate answer to "who you are"
To let you go, or let my imagination of us go,
Is not going to matter much in the grand scheme of your life
I can now accept that loving you will only slow you down
I can now accept that my love for you would be unreturned
I know how this goes
And I have already accepted the pain to follow
But I am thankful for all that you have come to teach me
It has been a joy
An amusement park ride that turned into a luxury cruise
I believed you could have been "the one"...
And if you are not,
I am just glad I was able to dream of loving you at all.

Seasons Change

Like the colors of autumn tree leaves, change is inevitable
                        I realize that now....
Summer....
If asked a year ago, I would have never believed that this season would
change. I would have told you differently. I would... have been wrong.
Hmm....
I would have said something like, "You are the only woman I could imagine
sharing my life with...." Like, "I dig you so much, I would give birth to your
children if scientifically or humanly possible."
Like, "Your smile resembles the sun in the west – the day must begin with
you."
But things are different now. Accepting that has been difficult; particularly
when every once in a while , the spark comes back for half a second, and
hope comes back for half a second, and the warm desire for the scent of
your hair and the breathy hypnotic reverberation you call a voice comes
back for a full second. But I recognize that two seconds of spark, hope and
warmth cannot recreate our connection. Because we used to be on the
same page, now we're in two different books. Even though we're still on
the same shelf of the library, it's just not the same.
                        And I realize that....

Autumn....
You know, friendship is an interesting thing. For some, it's cherished and
defended till the end. For others, it's only considered valuable if it's self-
serving. For those in the middle, friendship can be strong and fragile at
the same time. That was us - strong and fragile. At first – the beginning of
the season – I don't even think you liked me very much. We were brought
together through **happenstance** – we **happened** to befriend the same
people – the only reason why we were even seen together.
Then at some point...
            ... it was not strange to hear your name and mine in the same
sentence...
 then in the same breath....
 But like I said, ours was one that was partially fragile.
"Is there something wrong?" I should have been brave enough to ask. I
knew there was, but I thought you would tell me when you were ready.
You never did....

Silently fragile on both our ends; and now I have to ask every other person besides you to find out if you're okay... or busy... or alive. I should have tried to enjoy this season more while it lasted.

I realize that....

Winter....

I have this feeling that I disappointed you. I heard your tears and hesitated when I should have been certain - absolutely, I'll help you. Instead, I asked "what happened?" like you weren't going to tell me AFTER you heard me say "yes." But no... no, no, no, no... I have no idea what it took to ask... And the one person you trusted at that moment had the wrong answer, or at least didn't answer the way you wanted me to. And though you say now that it's okay, and even though it takes you three months to return a phone call... that has to be done at a particular time of day... and never on weekends... I don't believe you've forgiven me. But it is okay, winter was fun. I just didn't want it to end so quickly.

Spring....

Now I realize that I'm not immune to being on the wrong side of sensitivity.

Because, even if my cries aren't heard, I have to make sure I hear yours before they start. But I just can't anymore.

And even if it is not okay with you, it is okay with me. I hope you understand if I decide to move on before you let me go, but I don't want you to waste any energy trying to let me off nicely.

I know there will be no more two-hour phone calls or random e-mails for advice.

I have to be ready to not hear your quirky jokes and endearing chuckle.

I have to be ready to not see the way your eyes disappear when you smile.

I'll be ready... I'll be ready for the next season... I think this is going to be a good long summer.

Haiku Raw #1

I don't mind if you
Don't shave your legs; long as I
Don't get razor burned.

Haiku

Is it me, you or
Is it we that make this love
"Thang" comp-lic-a-ted?

Sensual

I wanted to greet you... brand new
Exceptional beauty
Gracing me with your life inquiries
Sitting beside each other
Expanding our minds together
Realizing that the sunrise is near
Our eyes get heavy
Heavy like your thoughts
Heavy like the rain when you leave town
Heavy
We move our less than heavy hands through our respective "naturals"
Appreciating our perfect imperfections
Knowing full well that we hardly ever get a chance to be...
Like this... like this
Sensually yours in mind, body, and spirit
I-I-I enjoy the vibrations of your voice as it relaxes in the quiet of the early
morning
Tingling my eardrums with every syllable
Chills across my skin on every intonation
Why leave this moment?
How unique our shades of brown, yet we match well
Caresses are light
Attempting to find a new comfort... with ourselves
A new introduction of familiar sites
Sharing us... we... again for the first time
Sensual motions without effort, without reservation
How else could we be but... like this?
Like this...
Slowly moving... still captive to the flow of our verbal exchanges
Feeling the moisture in our palms
Inhaling our chosen fragrances
Exploring all physical nuances to a rhythm created in our synchronized
twists and turns
Can you imagine it?
This moment... everlasting
This moment... permanently ours
Imagining everyday... together...
Like this... like this.

Queen

Let me tell you about this girl named Queen.
Queen is a type of girl that you mostly see in your dreams
Amazing and powerful, as her name would have you believe.
Her smile can light up any room, like the night skies are lit up by the moon.
Her skin is like chocolate – smooth and desirable.
Her physique is as fine as wine; her charisma is indefinable.
Tall, dark and lovely, possessed with a heart absent of malice.
Eyes that sparkle so bright, even the stars are jealous.
They say *behind* every good man there is a good woman.
But *beside* any king there is this unrivaled Queen.
Her intelligence is as great as the day is long, a voice that could enliven any song.
The way she walks emanates confidence.
The way she talks defines prominence.
She's the embodiment of the spirit of her powerful African ancestors.
A strength that exemplifies beauty
A possessed knowledge that the world has yet to discover.
When Queen enters a room, everyone stops what they're doing just to get a look.
When she leaves, all of them are out of air, for their breath she took.
Queen is a dynamic woman made up of many dimensions.
People look at her with an eye of astonishment, wondering if she can possibly have any imperfections.
Yes, this sister is as *bad* as you can dream.
But you should have figured that out when I told you her name is *Queen.*

Haiku (for Tupac Amaru Shakur)

This world is missing
A soldier; the song plays, but
There is no sound heard.

Haiku

The sight of your face
Brings back hard to forget dreams
Of eternal love.

Haiku

The lonely night is
Cold; I need your arms to be
My fire, my truth.

Haiku

Summer nights in you
Like swimming in the bluest
Of oceans, rivers.

Haiku

Part 1
Sitting here trying
Not to listen to this most
Melancholy groove.
        Part 2
Trying not to fall
In love with the voice on the
Other end of the box.

Trust Love

In trust
I leave love unconditional to myself
Because I know I am the only human who will love me
On my most attractive days
And in my most unattractive moments.
With ease, I'll love with skinned knees
With a heart torn apart
No part... ing of ways.
I trust that love will not always be easy
It may not always be clear.
It may even be hard to hold on to
Even when it seems ever so near.
Please trust that my love will be open and free
And enough to give in abundance.
My love has had to replenish itself constantly
Just to keep up with the losses.
And even as love is passed to me...
With restraints and reservations,
Time limits and expiration dates,
My love will be everlasting.

Shortly

Shortly, the rain will wash away what is left
Autumn's leaves will have disappeared
And the trees and streets will be left bare.
Walking slowly down newly dried sidewalks,
Hands in pocket
– touch, feel, memory –
It will all come back within a breath.
And shortly, breathtaking recollections
Will be less commanding of thoughts of
Love,
Flowers,
And those other pretty things
That become topics of your favorite
Valentine's Day cards.
Maybe it is by nature
That we desire nicely wrapped
Happy endings of unreserved intimacy
And passion
For eternal lengths.
But shortly, memory will relax its hold
Love and time will renew and realign
And the trees will bloom again.

A Poem for Kendrah D. – 'Get Familiar'

A collection of fire, love and unabashed womanhood
Wrapped in five feet and two inches
Get familiar
My "Lioness" spirit standing in the sunlight
Observing the jungle that is this insane world in need of love, passion
and more hugs
Healing the world through musical vibrations
Tuned into the singing colors
I am the descendant of strong queens and visionary mothers of
civilization
And you can have it verified by my noticeable cuteness and the
silhouette accentuated by the shape of my hips that I am a "grown-ass
woman" and I can do as I damn well please
So please believe that the scar you notice on my neck is a wound
acquired in the battle that is life, and I need no reminders of my own
mortality to reinvigorate my fearlessness and enjoyment in living
I'm a bad, bad woman
Get familiar
You might scream, "Who is this chick in the Donovan McNabb jersey?"
But beyond my love for Eagles green
My heart bleeds...
For better days past being the only bit of brown in a room full of pink
nipples
I'm burning Bush effigies
In the effort and hope of inspiring the future generations to think
outside of the box named
"Status Quo"
And I'll be the first avenger to break through the cardboard
Get familiar
Unafraid to speak loudly
Unafraid to be heard clearly
Happy, humble, powerful and free
My style – not yours
My imperfections – I let them be known
My mind is my own
Get familiar.

Conversations

I would like to speak with you
About the world
Not an "ordinary speak," but a community and familiar speak
Love speak
I would like to talk to you about the world.
Let's converse about the unknown and all we think we know and are told is true
Let's explore places in our minds left untouched in normal humans, because our verbal intercourse won't be complete until every nerve ending is sparked by the echo of our whispers.
Let me converse with you on this long morning walk through foot paths on brown dirt, red dirt, black soil.
Let us wax philosophically on some Bob Marley lyrics, and break into nostalgia over the sound of children at play, and speak lovingly of the gift of a visible sunrise at the perfect time.
Let's talk about our dreams and nightmares and cold sweats and sleepless nights and restless mornings.
Let us talk about our dreams and hopes and fears in this physical existence:
Our children's world free of disease;
Our eternal lessons from experiencing each other's presence;
One less day without realizing our passions.
Our words settle and surround our senses like the smell of jasmine captures any nose within 100 feet.
I hear you... Let's talk about the blues and magic... I feel you... Let's converse about our first crushes... I know you... Let us be our most free in this moment... two voices strong.

Yo' Chocolate

I've been wondering why I love to stare at you
And daydream about your face at the most random moments
I do know that as much as you adore mine,
It's yo' chocolate that is the sweetest temptation
YO' CHOCOLATE...
... that seems to stick to my lips just right
It must be yo' chocolate that spoils my dinner every night
Satisfying my sweet tooth with just a glare, a wink
A soft touch by your hand across my face
And my heart is locked in... with your keys
And I'm not eager for an early release
A lifetime in your love lockdown would be the only route for my redemption
I'm certain that there is no other delicacy I enjoy more
Because this is not just a preference or something I like
This is about something I love
YO' CHOCOLATE...
... has me always coming back for more
Even at times when I wonder if you're bad for my health
Even at times when I am sure you are bad for my heart
When your aftertaste is not as sweet, I still desire your fragrance
The sight of you is treasured by many
As I see these brothers stopping flat in their tracks when they walk by you
Yo' chocolate has them hypnotized and hungry
Drooling uncontrollably like Pavlov's canines at the sound of your rhythmic stroll
Hoping to be bold and brave enough to have even a small word with you,
They try to catch your attention in the most awkward ways
But they don't know that you never stop moving and catching up with you is near impossible
Yet it's even more impossible to withdraw from the magnetism of your mahogany
Seemingly calling me even when you're out of touch
Kicking the habit of wanting you... is not my desire.
I...
would like...
for us...
to melt...
in each other.

Renaissance Woman

I remember the first time I met LaTesha S.
It was a bright autumn afternoon on Mount Olympus Drive
A dining hall named "Graham" was our place of rendezvous
There were no noticeable witnesses of this moment to document our interactions
As we compared hometowns and dorm halls
And related in the way that Black folks do
At that moment we were *cool...*
Like a soft Syracuse breeze...
We were *cool...*
Since that day Ms. LaTesha introduced herself to me, I have seen her grow and grow
Almost ten years strong, I have seen her grow and grow and grow and grow...
I am proud of the woman she has become
This Renaissance woman
Daring to strike through the skies like **LIGHTNING**
I am proud of the woman she will be
A brand new brilliance
Brilliant femininity bestowed with the strength of her ancestor mothers and sisters
I know her *fire* well
I know her *tenderness* too
She is a real Original woman
I love her.

Haiku

Your lips, my lips, love
Who needs rules when there is no
Game to be played here.

Sensual pt. 2

In still wanting to greet you in a brand new way
Candles brighten the path to the place we last spoke...
Of long lost days and long found memories
You've returned like the rain in April...
Still heavy, even after a dry March...
Still... heavy...
And I thought I could get by without your heavy whispers in the dark
But I realize the lie that I had to tell myself in order to survive till this
day...
This night... so quiet until the volume that is you appeared
And I am caught up in the music that is your voice
Listening so intensely to the singing coming off your lips
I want to blank out all other sounds
But I am enticed to play just the right Sol Edler and Kuku love ballads to
set the mood
And it is true... I still have a thing for loving each and every one of your
perfect imperfections
From the way you interrupt every other sentence, to your extra-
sensitivity to the cold
I wait with high anticipation to feel your face pressed against mine
Your hands slowly caressing my back
As we reacquaint ourselves with each other's favorite things:
Favorite foods, favorite colors, favorite... touches
I almost forgot how ticklish you are, as I remember how I fell in love with
your laugh the first time I heard it... or maybe it was the second time,
because your beautiful silliness took me by surprise when we first met
Now, I would travel over troubled waters to hear your laugh in person
I want to know this feeling more often
The feeling of never feeling tired when I'm next to you
Talking about our dreams way past the sunrise
Reading each other's emotions through the looks in our eyes
As the glow of the early morning reflects off of your golden brown skin
I wonder how it would be...
How it could be...
Everyday... like this...
Like this.

Haiku (for Kelechi)

Genius and brilliance
Comes from outside of the box
Sit out in the sun.

Haiku (for Kayonia)

Like light bouncing off
The rain soaked tree leaf; I see
The warmth in your eyes.

Stand in Your Truth (LaTesha's poem)

My dear friend,
Stand in your truth
Stand in the glow of your mind
And let your greatness shine through.
The truth that I know of you is your audaciousness...
The audacity to be uniquely yourself in the face of opposition
Even if it is not considered conventional, you proceed on the road you believe will lead you to your destination
Within that audacity, you have found strength
A boldness that I hope you keep throughout your whole life.
My dear friend,
Stand by your gifts
All of your gifts... all of them
You have overcome so much, and your gifts will bring you through anything else that will come your way
All the journeys that you have encountered have given you new lessons to learn
You have learned so much, and now in the midst of your learning, you have been blessed to do some teaching.
So now what lies ahead of you?
Whatever it is, breathe lightly, because you are the excellence you dream to be
You are the dream of those who came before you
And so you are the truth they have been waiting to hear
Stand in the light.

Shining Star (Jada's poem)

Challenge the sun with your bright rays
The world is waiting for your light
Be unafraid to shine
Do not let fear of success be your greatest fight
Be brave enough to lead the way...
Through all the obstacles you may encounter on your journey
Be brave enough to lead...
Follow only **your** destiny
You are a brilliant shining star
Didn't they tell you?
As long as you know that you are
You don't need them to tell you
Be the greatness that you are meant to be
Be the shining star that all of the universe can see.

Haiku

Have we met before?
You remind me of loving
Eyes of past, future.

Haiku

Dark clouds as far as
The eyes can see, reminds me
Of thoughts of goodbye.

Haiku

In the cold of the
Rain, I am but a lost child
Searching for warmth, love.

You Are

Like a supernova,
When you enter – explosion
Warmth arises from your center...
I am caught, but I know it's not an illusion.
Like the rain... rain, rain, rain, fall on me.
Love rain... fall on me.
You are like the rain on a spring day.
Or like the dew on the tree leaves before dawn.
You are the aurora during the dusk.
You are likely to be the lightning that struck me dead...
However and forever, you are the only to resuscitate me, lovely.
 You are stunning.
The glory of your space is the compassion you neglect to waste.
The way you let those "ebony locks" flow;
You are my, "for every action there is an equal and opposite reaction."
Indulging in conspiracy theory of the origins of humanity
Beyond me... criticize the counterintelligence / F.B. EyeSpy
Spine tingling thoughts on liberation of the indigenous nations...
Reparations... Revolutions.
As you escape with Giovanni & Sanchez & Lorde.
Escape and reflect with Angelouuuuuu.
Escape with Baraka & Hughes & Wright
Preaching Malcolm & Assata & Angela tooooooo.
You are rhythm
Music
My favorite song on the soundtrack to my life.
You are the sound of Miles & Satchmo & Parker.
Smooth as Thelonious on the keys...
You are Lady Day's voice – Heaven.
Sparkle if you will.
Captivation is not the word.
It's Love.

Khrishnuku

Pisces. Sparkle. Light. INTENSE. Love.
Spirit. Star. Earth. Moon. **Ocean.**

River. Mountain. Fire. Flower.
Youth. **Wisdom.** Truth. **Powerful.**

Sassy. Strong. Sensual.

Warmth. LIGHTNING. **Thunder.**
Wind. Space.

Sun. Planet.

Goddess.
WOMAN.
WOMAN.
WOMAN.
Woman.

Haiku

Star crossed in... like; paused
In adoration for this
Defining moment.

Haiku

Little brown boy, why
Are you crying so blue? You
Can love and be loved.

Haiku

Friend, in your distress
I lost your trust in the dark
Of night. Forever?

Sweet Melody

I know this sound... I really do
It's that walking rhythm that reminds me of you
Gracefully attacking the ground with that diva sway
I can recognize it from a mile away
The sight of your gliding body is imprinted in my dreams
And it seems...
Nothing can make my mind tingle like shaking leaves...
Other than you
And it's true
You don't belong to me, even though I wish to belong to you
So, I hope you don't think about stoppin'
Put a little extra twist in those hips, 'cause you know I watchin'
(Ain't that what 2Pac said? Word!)
Forget the singing birds; I want to wake you up every morning to that sound...
Yeah, oh yeah...
I would love to place a crown on your majestic golden brown... head... yeah
Oh, to hear your charming voice, I'm fed...
By your refined "twang"
Like the favorite song I sang in school
You are a melodious jewel
Ain't nothing sour about you
You are the sweetest taboo
But hopefully not forbidden fruit
'cause shoot,
I just want to be lucky enough to exclusively listen to your groove, if only for a season
And I jump at any excuse or reason
To hear that precise note
Only you can create
Play it for me again
Play it for me again.

Haiku Raw #2

Sweat heavy, hips thrust
Squeeze those thighs 'round my waist; girl,
Can I be your star?

The Other Man

I don't mind being the other man…
For you…
I don't mind waiting till you come up with an excuse to tell him
While I wait for the call that says you're coming over
And I know it's wrong
I know how much this could hurt him
Because I've been "the man" who didn't realize there was "another man"
I've spent a cold night alone while my Eve was kept warm by another Adam
And now here I am…
Yours on the side
I even remember the first time we met - he introduced us…
If he only knew…
How he brought me to you…
How he brought your heart to mine…
Now everyone seems to know about us except him
But I don't know if I care what my friends say
I know I don't care what your friends say
All I know is that I want to be wanted
I want to have someone to fill this emptiness
And just because you're with him doesn't mean I have to be without you
I know you can't stay longer
Even though I ask you every time
I know you won't leave him
That's why I never ask
I know you love him
Because I can feel it
He loves you too
But I know he's getting suspicious…
He tells me all the time.

Haiku

Four year itch from you
Missing dysfunction is strange
Nothing new for us.

Haiku

> Part 1
I can pretend well
Like I don't care that you found
Another, but no.
> Part 2
I am broken in
Several pieces; bad dreams
Of your chilled embrace.

No More Mister Love Poem

You want to talk?
According to you, things have changed
Not just a little, but totally rearranged
A shell of what it used to be
Yeah, I remember that – you & me
Of course, if it was that cool, our thing never would have...
Become "formerly known as"
Or, "no longer chillin'
With mi bella villain"
But you scorched me when I thought I was invincible
Broke and burned my heart... unbelievable
And now you want to be friends...
With me...
Really?
Why are you trying to act like nothing ever happened?
Like I imagined it all.... I dreamed these emotional scars to be dampened
No St. Valentine's message here
Forget about Christmas; we didn't even make it to the New Year
Understand that when you see me, "Pain" has been living in my guestroom
Unfortunately for you, "Love" hasn't lived here since June.

Haiku (for the single mother)

Can a woman raise
A man in lands of hard knocks?
She had to. Thank you.

A Promise to my Future Child

Welcome to the world
You are the life that I will hold so dear to me
The beauty for which all the universe and I can see
I write this to you in order to give you faith that I will always be there
A shield when you need it, your blanket of care
The happiness that your birth brings me is unexplainable
The creation of life... the witnessing of a miracle
As this world shows its faults, you may see things that may not please
you
The world can be dangerous, like an unfenced zoo
But do not overlook the beautiful things
The flowers blooming as the birds sing
The puffy white snow
The appearance of a rainbow
You are my heart, my precious dove
You are my guiding light through a tunnel of appreciation, giving and
love
Every time you speak, walk, or smile, I'll know just how blessed I am
Every time you look at my face, hear my voice, or make me smile, you'll
know how happy I am
This is my promise that you can always count on me
I will be with you as long as forever might be
The things we'll go through will be challenges we'll face together
In a sense, like a bird and its feathers
When these challenges come, who knows what we'll do
Just remember that through it all, I will always love you.

I have a new story to tell (Sio'bhan's poem)

Look at me
Tell me what comes to your mind?
Be honest
What labels would you like to place on me?
What kind of box do you want to put me in?
I accepted all of your limited expectations...
And I have lived them all
But I have a new story to **live**
And I have a new story to **tell**
My new story is about fighting the fight that I thought wasn't mine
The fight to dream beyond the obstacles put in front of me...
And those obstacles I put in front of myself
My new story...
 is about believing...

in my greatness...

in my strength...

And right now...
Right at this very moment, I've decided to do something new and different
 I've decided to walk a different path leading to a different destination -
Freedom.
And I can tell that you may find this new story hard to believe
But I have the scars to prove it
And the mind and heart to survive and thrive in it
I have this brand new story I want to tell you
And it begins by ending old ways of treating myself
And starting fresh ways of looking at my life
This story is about a girl finding a new road to her womanhood...
A journey she didn't know she had the courage to endure
I'm here to share this new story with you and anyone else who will listen
I will not be in fear of success, and I am now brave enough to live it.

Haiku

No time for feign pride
And constricted attempts at
Loving; dive in bare.

Scorpio

Water sign
Compatible with Cancer, Pisces & Virgo
Stream-lined
Infamously known for his passionate spirit and spunky libido.
Luminous moon over the horizon calls your name
Captured by your intrinsic groove, you can't hear the vibe
As confused as most, I have trouble with the same
But I'm here in the shadow of your afterglow – live.
Dampened by the melancholy
Or enlightened by the revelry
Caught hesitant to float on the rivers lit by the rays of the morn
Openly stinging crush, falling backward over Gemini and Capricorn.
The groove is off....
The stars must be aligned wrong
If you ask me, they've always been like an awkward song
Drowning in lunar-inspired high waves
Love notes masked by the writing on the walls of caves
Turned sideways, the lines not to be crossed seem to disappear
All barriers gone; a caress in nothing – nothing to fear.
References to a warm touch on a cold day
Innocent voyages coming into play
Tingling finger
Tingling toes
The night sky only sparkles and glows...
For the lovers who rock!
Design the signs
Don't ask mine
Star-crossed insanity as an excuse for the crime
Take me back to when time seemed infinite
A time with no *time limits*
When it was no matter if water matched with air or earth with fire
All that mattered... all we cared was that one desire:
Unforgiving happiness.

III
Can a Poem Kill AND Give Life

Can a Poem Kill?

Can a poem kill?
Can I stab the oppressor with a verb?
Kick him with a noun?
Strangle him with an adjective?
Blow out his brains with a metaphor?
Can my timed rhymes destroy the mystique of his blond hair and blue
eyes?
Completely eradicating his dominating hold on society
Don't need a gun
My mind is fully loaded
My pen is aimed and ready to fire
A poem... Kill?
May
I
Slay
The Conductor of
The
"Slave"
Trade
And
Master of
The "Slave"?
Can I poke John Smith who poked Pocahontas, and screwed "hers" and
"mine"?
Kill?
Linguistically assassinate those who found legality to segregate
Poetically bury alive the architect of Apartheid
Verbal annihilation of the participants of colonization
Concise and killer euphemisms to rebel against the famous
"-isms"(Sexism, Racism, Classism)
Can the words on the page incite my people to rage?
Can my words show everyone that it's not "his world"?
Can I hold this poem to his head, having him beg for mercy?
Can it kill?
A poem... Yeah!

Reality Check

Unity looks bleak in the street
We pose when we meet / the more
We live the struggle, the harder we beef
Liberation... looks like a slim hope
Freedom beyond the scope
Of those we call adult / scream revolt
Just thought of as naïveté
And ignorance / simple insignificance
Conceived from devilish influence
How do you do it? –
Turn dissent into betrayal / cash-bought degree from Yale?
Secrets behind the veil... of deception
Of course you forgot to mention...
That little incident in college
"No crime without the knowledge"
Cease with all the garbage...
That you've been throwin'
Purposely foregoin' / all the
Deception you've been knowin'
Disregard that we're fed
Gross inconsistencies / vast irregularities
About the current stage and history
Desire deliverance from this misery
With all that's going on,
We forget to raise each other
Instead of conversing like sister/brother
We curse family like perfect strangers
Not knowing the danger... of furthering
The Lynch plan
We can't OVER-stand
If we don't see the UNDERhand...
Rules used against us / they call
And we fall to rush / like domesticated animals
Mis-educated of the intangibles...
By schools of mediocrity / reproduce the

Oppressive tools in uniformity / young people
Lost in cages of monotony
Still trying to figure out if we're the victims
Or the perpetrators / pain now for the victim,
Promise the "perp" the treasure later
But later never arrives / fall in-full and fall in-line
Assist bringing down your brethren on a lie
Cry mighty people cry
(Cry, cry, cry)
I applaud you for the elevation you seek
Continue to reach
Till the mountain reaches its peak
All-in-all, when you study, do more than repeat
We repeat the mistakes of the enslaved,
Physically and mentally
Slave to the catechisms on
"Black inferior" ideology
Following televangelist primetime
Hypocrisy / You may realize the duplicity of the system
Choose the donkey or the elephant
Still end up as the victim / two parties
Two choices / neither really hear the voices
They just play the vote and game the people
Like "toyses" / and it "annoyses" me
Seeing people fall for the ploys and schemes
Attracted and hypnotized by the "American dreams"
But isn't all a lie? / The few are let to make it
The rest suffer and die
The new Uncle Thomas has PhD and JD
Attached to his name / just a part of the game
Creating bourgeois soldiers to keep the masses in place
A superior sub-race? – You're led to believe
A common sense thief
Cutting your people at the knees
"The man" you appease
Forgot all the basics
Mind wasted / terminally delusional
Can't heal nine face lifts

Six bags of horse hair in your basement
Did I "let the cat out of the bag"?
I thought it was just a fad
Looking like a clown, I thought you were glad
Let's talk about your business
Press-on nails on your sale list
Silicon injections for your thin lips
And that's just for morning jog trips
Trying to attain white supremacist
Standards of beauty / nothing truly...
Remaining from the time you were a newbie
Conditioned to believe our people
Come from UNcivilization
Degeneration / praised and practiced
Across the nations / not over-standing that our
People created knowledge
Only to fall prey to the promise
Of reciprocity from the hobgoblins
Manipulators / control the world by
Becoming people traders
Massacre orchestrators
Steal from the original innovators
The true knowledge is in vapor
We are progeny of the loss
What's the cost... of the confusion?
"Bling-bling" and hoe- illusions
Are passed in our muses
We applaud this insanity
Apathetic conformity
To make comfort for the "majority"
Long to see... a vision
Not poisoned by assimilating intuitions
Into remission / we must achieve
My people breathe... common sense
Into life, please / be nonsense realizers
Truth advisers / for your siblings and your children
Tell them the establishments a muck / filthy and corrupt
Advising billion dollar tax cuts / for the rich

Still making me sick / making me hurl
To view the world... as it is today
Bemused in the way... to find a safe place
Injustice continues / 21st century lynchings –
Shootouts in apartment venues
When will the masses stand to challenge all the wrongs?
Sitting down just makes the infringements strong
Goal of domination and knew it all along
Stolen elections headquartered from a farm
The people blinded by fear like fog
Remember Marvin and ask "What's going on?"

Haiku

Madness, destruction
Who's making intelligent
Fools the world's leaders?

My Revolution Has a Cause

My revolution has a cause
I said, myyyyyyyy revolution has a cause
And excuse me if I don't pause
For your applause
But I am too lost in the charge
To be sorry for my impolite barge
Attacking the world's social *faux pas*
With another poetic clause
And another poetic clause
And even when you're close to lost
It's laid on you one more time like a wicked left cross.
Because my re / vo / lu / tion has a cause
So don't try to hide those in charge
Of keeping my people encaged behind mind weakening bars
`Cause all your kindness - it's just a farce
It's just a farce!
Unfortunately taught to believe that you're the superstars
In this game of life and laws
Just other victims, more privileged than ours
But "when the truck comes," it will come for us with sharp claws
And you'll be safe in the back, playing the "reverse race card."
And my revolution has a cause.
While you use the word to get applause
I use it for liberation of the people, gods
Your dreams of shiny racecars
Didn't prepare you for the justice wars?
And you just realized that "Leave It to Beaver" was just a farce
Just a farce
Come to far
To lie down while the dust collects and covers my limbs like gauze
Pseudo-leadership with concerns that don't match ours
False alliances undeserving of our trustful thoughts
Believing you can make a difference with giving token awards
And now you want to relay commercial messages, so you want me to pause?

Nah, because my revolution has a cause
And when the revolution comes, we will not apologize for causing your alarms
With another poetic clause
And another prophetic clause.

Haiku

If this is karma,
What does the next century
Hold for down-pressers?

Put on Your Glasses for '07

I know you're not blind / so put on your glasses / you're running out of time / better make it the fastest / they say dust to dust / & ashes to ashes / got deluded by the system / so you trip on the masses

Smiling on the surface / who knew it would've lasted / making love to currency / infatuated with plastic / freedom on layaway / invested in gasses / got the truth on hold / it always got there the "lastest" / wannabe "Ghetto Supastar" like Pras' asses / lost in the translation / I'll interpret for you slackers / we're still slave to the perpetrators of the middle passage / scared to escape / let's exercise these "Harriet Tubmanastics" / lynchings more discreet / now through lethal injection practice

But I know you're not blind / so put on your glasses / got 24 inch rims on your car / but your life is so tragic / kill your brother for a Northface - his life for an over-priced jacket / I'm all out of patience / you ain't getting no more passes

The message of war blown through trumpets / Clarence and Condoleezza puppets / masking all the facts – these reality nuggets / Black and Latino reservations / slumlord nightmares in the projects / brothers acting like rivals / caught up in the madness / bombs over Baghdad, nuclear pundits / reflecting the stupidity of their so-called leaders / stubborn idealists acting in the favor of corporate overseers / the war on terrorism not what it appears / debts to the original descendants / centuries in arrears / political positions planned / guided by irrational fears

But you're not blind / better put on your glasses / he's gettin' out of line / hurry before he crashes / let him get away with being a fool / a blundering fascist / we got the talk straight / let's put it into practice

Celebrity addictions dominating the news / got genocidal conditions being financed by your jewels / Stalking Britney's baldness; Angelina and Brad / Madonna buying African babies / while Sudanese refugees pour into Chad / confused by the coverage / you retreat into a hole / bind your hands and feet / hang yourself from a pole / but you saw that coming / cause you had on your glasses / paid attention to the clues / didn't get lost in the grasses / ashes to ashes / & dust to dust / How are they gonna cope when we start calling their bluff?

Practicality

Pardon my impracticality / I was too caught up in empathy / to be the usual / or what is usually the case / with the many I see around me / advancing these pseudo-intellectual notions of progress / mindless... drones for the gringos on the hill / butt-kissing and bootlicking / so the already tense waters of conformity don't spill... over / and we are found... out / "Because we have to be practical" / but I'm partially partial to what is revolutionary / and bear with me / If I seem to be / cursed by naïveté / and practically ignorant of what is supposed to be considered glory.

Because glory to me is not a large check with a white man's signature on it apparently validating my existence / glory to me is freedom to think from the outside. Glory to me is not seeing myself through the eyes of others / glory to me is knowing the value of my own beauty. Glory is not being a neo-slave / glory is liberation – old and new.

So excuse me if I believe that people like you need people like me / because WE keep things moving / and I know "practicals" and "impracticals" are necessary to each other in order to make progress possible / but don't expect me to go along with the already over-prescribed program / to your inconvenience, "the good Negro complex" must have skipped a few generations / and I am the embodiment of a "slave insurrection" / so / I / will / continue / to / let / my /Afro / glow / and I'll excuse you if you didn't know / that all my 400 years without a comb / could never drive me to commit Madam C.J. Walker's formula to the wool on my dome / so I'll leave the activator for the viscosity in my carburetor / and I'll rock it natural like Garvey prophesized / the more kinks I grow in my hair, the less kinks I have in my mind / so, if I'm too practically impractical for you to stomach – GOOD / that means I rep the rebels like I should / so let it be known, there is no such thing as practical freedom / liberation only comes from people willing to attain it by being a little impractical.

Haiku

Fifty long shots in
The dark; the Bell tolls for Sean
While blood stains the badge.

SLAVE TO REALITY

Change reality
Slave to reality
Aware of reality
Master your reality
Soldier of reinvention
Soldier of dreams cast in lights of disdain
Black prophets beside street lights and yield signs
Don't sigh... at my apparent naïveté
No ignorance to bliss
Ain't this...
Turning off radio boxes providing faux lyrical muffins without the creamy filling of Melle Mel substance, Rakim funkness, Tupac revolutionary thugness
"Because I'm from the gutter and I'm still here"
Must this...
Be how it has to?
When all is said and done
Are those Cocoas that say that being educated is acting white, the same as those Cocoas that make major life decisions based on an approval of whites?
Make nice like Steppin' Fetchit
To get this
Imaginary seat at the table
In the 21st century, unable
To break chains
But break fast with blames
In outward directions
Reflections necessary
Blessed are those with the patience to listen to the monotony
And not lose faith in the family
Like neglected 15 year old mothers
Hustlin' on the hope that there is a way past societal expectations for little brown girls beatin' the concrete on Reebok-warmed tired feet
And I concede that I can't see past tomorrow without thinking about yesterday's sorrow
I bleed hope, but scab anger
At those who want to limit my mind or the length of my 'fro

I don't know, please believe I don't know, why Brothas look at other Brothas with stares of rivalry and hate instead of respect and love
And I don't know, please believe I don't know, why Brothas see other Brothas as enemies instead of as family
And let me be the first one to say that I don't like bowties and brown suits as my wardrobe of choice for the new revolution
And screw Starbucks and these other Corporate Caucasian missionaries
Trying to save our souls from eternal damnation of buying our own shit
To guide us on a holy path towards salvation and everlasting love of Jesus Christmas sale blowout mocha latte
And I don't get excited about how many Black CEO's there are - I want change!
Beauty is skin deep, but I can't get my beauty sleep
With these dreams rolling in my head
That Black Power is dead
A mental suicide the coroner's office said
And how can I not believe him when the evidence is staring in my face
Young, gifted and Black – look at the world that awaits you
And if we are so brilliant, so amazing, why are we *slaves to reality?*
If we are so powerful, so strong, why do we pose and wear masks to fit in a place made available for the best performance of conformance?
How could there be any delusions that there are not bullets flying outside aiming for our minds?
Where are the soldiers of change willing to be seen and heard?
Being a soldier doesn't pay well and I am concerned that we have found heroism in exploitation
I'm hoping for a more hopeful revelation
But how will we liberate if we are given low valued expectations?
Some say I dream too much
But I say I need to dream better
Why leave ourselves with broken spirits?

Sellouts with Guns

WAR!!!
Between the blood on the streets
And the dead bodies lying on the ground,
That's what you would believe
War!!!
And this is not a third world country you're viewing
Oh, with the 14 and 15 year olds armed for battle
This is right in your own backyard
Sellouts with guns
Self-destruction
Self-worthless
Selfishness... encapsulated in cold steel
Packing heat to fill the insides of so-called "enemies" with hollow points
Tag teaming with the local big city police department to bring domestic terrorism to the people's village
And to compound the stupidity,
You lift up your shirt to show the "gloc" so well tucked in the waist of your pants
But I realize the youth and ignorance of your mind,
As you pose a stance to convey dominance,
But have a high-powered weapon aimed in the direction of your testicles
Dangerous species, I know you well
Feeling that you need to feed on the despair of others to feed yourself
Raw survival is your only concern
The condition of your people – a secondary matter
Forget the brothers with bowties arm-in-arm with white women
Sellouts are created in your image
Instead of dancing, diming, and shucking and jiving for the man
You execute your own people for the benefit of white thought
You are a skunk in lion's clothing.

Haiku (for the "Jena 6")

part 1

Nooses and whyte masks
Hang from the tree. Charlie sees small
Prank. I see Ku Klux.

part 2

Six in Jena, caged
By judicial lynchings thought
Passé since **_Brown_** days.

part 3

Whyte "just-us" served, like
You promised - with the stroke of
Your pen. Lives ruined.

part 4

Tennis shoe as a
Weapon??? Makes me wanna holla
No peers as jurors.

What it is

So this is what war is.
Silence...
There are no smiles to heal the pains
Pains in the hearts of the wise
The pains in the hearts of the young and innocent
Just a real hard pain, not the usual throbbing when you burn your hand
on the pot on the stove...
Something different
Something you can't seem to define
So this is what war is
Tears...
Only sounds of sobs break the calm
Crying – if only to break the continued motionlessness of the moment
Cries of mothers and fathers grieving for their children
Sons and daughters crying for their mommies and daddies...
Endless
War? Is that how you heal this?
Life lost...
Lost because someone forgot its worth
Forgot that there is more to it than meaningless pride
No more joy
No more of that look of hope... for peace
Only anger left
Only vengeance on the minds of men
No thinking, just retaliation, supposedly in the name and honor of the
slain
Senselessness...
So this is what war is.

Don't Wanna be Scared of Brothas

You pulled up fast and took away my safety
Daylight drive-bys, what's up with us lately?
And now I'm looking for a reason to blow
You reap what you sow
But why all this self-hatred so close to my home?
Progress so slow
Stagnation never seems to get old
We better be wary of the garbage we're told
Tell me, how do we make these decisions?
Who is making these rules? Got us jumping out of bridges
Poison schemes / poised to kill our dreams
Things are never, ever, ever, ever really what they seem
I'm on my way back to the future
Where we speak in rhymes and love songs by Luther
No Berettas or tech nines
Just music and soul train lines
We have our minds on peace and peace on our minds
But being a Black man is a dangerous occupation
In a nation where we pay no attention to the obstacles we're facing
So we're caged and we respond like animals
When released, we prey on our fam like jackals
So we look to the outside to save ourselves
From the pain of even living with ourselves
Still a danger to the health of our necks
Bullets and beat-downs from those who are supposed to serve and protect
Caught the effect
Listening and praising wannabe gangsters
Modeling to our children to be glorified slaves, instead of their own masters.
I don't wanna be scared of brothas
I'm tired of people telling me to fear my brothas
Why die to get rich?
Trying to make it fit
Suspects in our own deaths / why do we match half of the fingerprints?
Last night, I thought I heard the voice of Malcolm
Screaming about how we need to free ourselves from the bedlam

Back to this current event
Burned in my memory, living it again and again
Wrong place, wrong time, they say it again
They destroyed, I have to rebuild and make amends
Masking your shame
Stories of jacking to bolster your name
I can still see your eyes, praying for God to erase it
It might be tough, but I'll face it.

Corporate Sponsored Revolutions

The enemy has a new disguise in his hands
With Starbucks uniforms and Old Navy cargo pants
Construction plans without chocolate residents
Call me a menace
But I think they want our streets to be replenished
Repopulated with Wal-Mart and Target, instead of corner markets
It's madness to think that's the only way *el barrio* can profit
No logic in city council
But I've already said a mouthful
About these corporate sponsored revolutionaries.
Buying out the brown to promote the scam
Land grab, more sophisticated then when they jacked Manhattan
You did it to the Natives back in the day
Selling cheap trinkets or letting the bullets spray
A new day is here
But a new plan to fear
Fully gentrified by the end of the year
Stuck is complacency
Following blindly
While corporate machines disregard the community
Fooled into slaving for minimum wage
Falling for the tricks, I thought we turned that page
So now we hear talk about redeveloping the 'hood
The money's good
So we bend over for the burnt wood
Imperialists of the ghetto got us deceived
That the less of us around, the safer we'll be.

The Realness

To see what's left in your life,
Wondering why your whole
World is coming apart due to
A lie. This is the realness:
The infatuation, the
Miscommunication, Jay's
Words giving you the
Realization; the burning bed
The murdered dead, the held-
up feelings that you never
Said; the way you left it, the
No exception epic, the piss in
The corner Nick, the killer "hick"
Flick, the below the belt favor
Lick; as I arrive as the originator,
The crowd motivator, the
Ignorance terminator, the mind's
Incubator, the *believe in lover*,
The mass-velocity-acceleration
Calculator; the poetic
Ambassador of the future,
The graphic story teller, the
Truth/never liar; it's coming to you
Through the profiler; you still the
Crack dealer? The skill stealer?
The common copier? The fake
Player? The wannabe
Challenger? The "real killer"?
The only person you ever scared
Was your teeny brother, your
Yes proclaimer, your in the closet
Lover, the only one who could ever
Understand ya'; weird as it might be,
Imitation is your greatest creation,
Movement of the world halted by
Your "keepin' it real" idealization;
The dead-beat fathers, the extra-

marital lovers, the child abusers,
The heroine users, the wife beaters,
The exhale but didn't inhale swearers;
The celebrity stalkers, the whining
Walkers, the close-minded talkers,
Daring to write *swastika* symbols
With magic markers; the alcoholics,
The drunk drivers, the gun addicts,
The suicide divers, the ill-advisers;
The fire starters, the tabloid reporters,
The serial murderers; the chain
Smokers, thinking they're not
Living longer, but not knowing they're
Dying slower; the needle sharers, the
Disease spreaders, the no condom
Wearers, the "I can't feel anything"
Whiners; the pessimistic few, the
Apocalyptic view, the disregard
Of children news; how the world
Has changed, since your business is
No longer private, it's just part of
The game; the TMZ reports, the
People's Court, the National
Inquirer, the Gossip Show wire,
The president bashing, Fox News'
Mind-polluting, the justice system
Thrashing; the unending war, the
Hungry poor, the asking for more,
Destroyed by a ruthless core; you
Go on and on about who you want
To blame the world's
Imperfections on; the lying, the
Crying, the ear biting; OJ used
To be free, an incompetent jury,
Another nationality; it's never good
Enough for your version of the story;
The fact is you see only what you
Want to see; the white sheets and
Hoods are a testament of your
Blank mind, the lack of power you
Possess due to your acceptance of

Solely your "own kind;" the people
Say it, you never hear it; at first you
Loved it, now you hate it; the world
Is open, the children know it, the
Music is playing, the people are
Embracing, the noise is stopping;
The thing that's left is your final
Breath; until this ends, we'll wait
Till then.
Now, how easy is this?

Haiku (for Obama)

Obama!!! Believe!!!
Pundit lies cannot rule; dream
Bigger than right wing.

Contemplate

Have you ever contemplated suicide when the flowerless sidewalks and the "brick housings" aren`t enough? Contemplate the ideas left unfulfilled by Nat Turner - blood rushing down those white picket fences. Drying to cold purple stains.

Contemplation of liberating the people from their physical, psychological, and ideological imprisonment. While... I... sit in my own thoughts, forgetting the outside; only remembering the inner rage, I contemplate. I contemplate the reliving of pain of an entire people. Do I have the strength? What have I done that compares to... everything? Nothing... I can only sit here and contemplate... my next move... my next step... my next stand... my next movement....

Uncle Dubya'

Uncle Dubya', Uncle Dubya'
The drunken descendent of
Uncle Sam
Trying to be the master of the land
And the savior of others
Bullets and bombs are your rose petals
Spread across adolescent beds
Calculated domestic fear mongering
To propagate your agenda
Just politics as usual
While the media emphasizes the lack of approval
Maybe you are the perfect president
Protecting Caucasoid privilege
And patriarchy
Imprisoning those opposed to the empire
And maybe the "founding fathers"
Would applaud your "re-selection" as commander-in-stupidity
Because reality tells me
That the "trickle-down" theory
Is parallel to Jim Crow
And by the time you understood that
You missed the irony of people waving
American flags on the top of roofs
Floating over flooded streets
With chalk written pleas of
"Help me!"
"Help me!"
Remember me?!
Because poverty provided a perfect cloak
Of invisibility
And as outlandish as it was
I couldn't believe her
When she said Condoleezza
Had time for a shoe sale
And I'm reminded that
Many of us are partly to blame
For allowing you to use "9/11"

As your personal excuse card.
Torture?!
9/11
War for oil?!
9/11
Racial profiling?!
9/11, baby!
Too many were slaves to your illusions
Caught up in national security delusions
With no demands for solutions
To why bible pimps and corporate dogs
Have well-dressed puppets making laws on the hill.
So Uncle Dubya', Uncle Dubya'
I can see through the veil of deception
That has been weaved in your favor
And now understand the plans behind
Your father's CIA favors
Eight is enough.

Stand Up

Belly rolling laughter rumbling through the halls
Heart stopping rage when you caught the pause.
Unbridled wickedness of unabashed jealousies
Compassionate whispers relegated to memories.
Kitchen-knife cuts up and down your back
Razorblade incisions around your wrist in fact.
Lies and deceit broadcast from your summer farm
Our non-conformist appearance causing alarm.
~ Rebels and Artists, Stand up! Zombies and Clones, sit down ~
Draped in misery as you claimed your fame
False histories enforced your game.
You tried it all in college, walked with the 'caine
"Coked up" mentality, now war you maintain.
Experimenting with acid – you're feeling kinda' funny
Waking up to the dream of being a crash-test dummy.
~ Rebels and Artists, Stand up! Zombies and Clones, sit down ~
Raising young minds to fall to the bottom
"Keep yourself in check, or have a fate like Sodom."
Nonsense and self-hate are being fed to you
Accept and pass on, because you don't know what else to do.
Delusional in your quest for external acceptance
The pain and the shame have been somewhat relentless.
Trapped by false treasures promised in posh images
Led astray to the edge before this stanza finishes.
Now you wish the world to be covered in drones and bombs
Hold your friends and enemies by the top of their palms.
Consent to the usual, you sit back and partake
You won't stand and break the silence for your own sake.
~ Rebels and Artists, Stand up! Zombies and clones, sit down ~

Haiku

Image is nothing
Break free of Wall Street shackles
Meek souls will rule days.

On November 4, 2008

There are still remnants of the energy and joy I felt that night
The absolute amazement on my face could not be explained when...
At 11:00pm Eastern time, the national news programs declared that he won...
Barack Obama was elected President of the United States.
"I can't believe it."
With tears in my eyes...
"I can't believe it."
And even though I believed the day would come,
The reality was still a shock to the system
So thankful to see this day.
So grateful to feel this moment.
Obama! Obama!
He stands on the hopes, dreams and prayers of those who came before him and before me.
Every march... every boycott... every stand made when society said to sit down...
That energy and that spirit holds us up and holds up this moment.
Obama! Obama!
Might this man change the direction of the world?
Or at least the way the rest of the world looks at America?
America is not always popular across the globe,
But the globe takes notice of what America does
And America did good that day.
Maybe, just maybe those truths are self-evident
And America believes all men really are created equal.
The tears of thousands on television and the tears of my own mother confirm...
How much this means to my people...
How much it shows that my people can do anything.
We have given birth to greatness.
I wanted to grab every Black child on the street and ask, "Do you believe now?"
Do you believe that you and your people can create greatness, no matter the odds?
In the words of Malcolm, "What do we care about odds?"

What were the odds Nelson Mandela could become president of South Africa?

What were the odds that Harriet Tubman could lead thousands of the enslaved to freedom?

"What do we care about odds?"

What were the odds that enslaved Africans would build a "White House" that 200 years later would house an African American president?

Blasphemy

Opposing the establishment
Governmental irrelevance
Suppression of the masses
Achieved through covert counterintelligence
Appalled that I don't imagine Buddha,
Jesus and Muhammad with straight hair and light skin,
But with bronzed melanin,
Dreadlocks and afro-puffs
Because that's blasphemy and blasphemous
Beyond rational
Cantankerous
The Klan and Neo Nazi's are after us
The good ol' boys club is not enough.
Dare to ask questions
Stand by the lessons
Explore more than the usual answers
Prepare for convalescence
Search the hidden truths
In these labyrinths concealed in suppressive pine
Save the world with one rhyme
Can you save the world with just one rhyme?
Lives cut up in pieces
The purpose of this poetic thesis
Spit fire in the cuts and creases
Won't end till the injustice ceases
Leave the Enemy playing in his own feces.
Blasphemy.
When will it be learned?
"War is not the answer"
Eventually, we'll get burned
By these ideological cancers
War-mongers
Election stealers
Political dissenters snuffed
When will we rebuff?

Enough is enough
Too many people in power betraying the people's trust.
Mr. Clarence Thomas, Ms. Condi Rice
You don't seem to understand your people's strife
Relaxing in the prominence of your high positions
Perfect examples of well-timed tokenism.
It's all a game
Create delusions of being awarded the same
It's more like a travesty...
If you all are what our kids should dream to be
Hoodwinked.
Bamboozled.
Blasphemy.
Now, who ordered the buffoonery with fries?
We seem to eat it up like cheese and we're mice
With all the stupidity that our music videos provide
Who would think we still have control of our lives?
One hundred fair-skinned women in one room
It must be the perfect Black male dream
Because those images we can't seem to help consume
Walking around, calling ourselves thugs
Staring each other down with angry mugs
Falling in line with the stereotypical concept
The Black man – self-destructive, sex-crazed and mentally inept
Frontin' like you still represent the streets
I didn't know the ghetto reached the Hills of Beverly
BET broadcasts just the way they want to see us
Violating each other; self respect be bust
Just puppets in the show; no worry, no fuss
Shut it all down
Destroy and rebuild is a must.
But that's blasphemy and blasphemous
Beyond rational
Cantankerous
The red state rulers are after us
Apparently the coast states aren't American enough.
Abolish affirmative action?
More like majority overreaction

Never mind reparations
Many fear the meaning of that compensation
And it cannot be put in better context
To understand that present-day enslavement is alive in the prison industrial complex
Unintelligently conforming to an arc of supremacy
Rooted in the ills of society
Stop.
Look.
Listen.
Rebellion.
Blasphemy.

Haiku

Who's invited to
Your "Tea Party"? Seems David
Duke's babies got loose.

Dream

I don't get to sleep as much as I want to
But I still have dreams
I dream of days when common sense will be used more often
When words of dissent will not be hypocritically construed as threats to
national security
I dream of a time when my people will be unafraid to be who they are
Blackness will be more than color
More than an alternative to whiteness
More than a history month
More than a degrading music video
And much more than a paragraph in a history textbook
My dreams have brothas and sistas who want to wear their hair natural
doing it without fear
Not because it's a fad
But because we have broken free
Free to have our own standards of beauty
Free to be alive and in love with the shades, curls and curves of our own
features
I dream of sharing my life with someone who has a mind that makes me
revere her every thought
And admire the sound of her voice
I dream of her spirit being one that empowers me
Making her strength all the more enchanting
I can see the beauty of the world when I look into her eyes
Her smile brings light to any dark day
I dream of her...
I dream of a day when my children will not be ashamed to have names
that may sound "too ethnic"
I dream that my children will learn all about themselves and their people
And will not be afraid of themselves and their people
I dream of a day when Africans of the continent and Africans of the
Diaspora will see how related we really are
I dream of seeing all Africans uniting for liberation of themselves and the
world

I dream of a day when I will be able to return to the mother continent
and discover my roots
I dream of new ideas
I dream of new perspectives
I dream of a new day
And I dream that I will live long enough to see it
But that is only a dream.

Haiku

There are those who see
Limits and change to fit in
Some make change fit them.

Toussaint's People

Who tells your story and why do they tell it? Who listens to your voices and why do they listen? Proud, proud Africans, do they tell your story the way it should be told? Or is it the same old, same old? *Ayiti* tell them... tell them of your rebellion. Tell them of your taking freedom from the jaws of slavery. Apparently unimaginable, because senile televangelists tell old Napoleon tales of you making deals with the devil. Tell them of your glorious heritage... that you were the shining guide to Black liberation... an independent African nation rivaling that other independent nation in the western hemisphere born a couple decades earlier. *L'Union Fait La Force* - and your strength has survived attacks upon your unity in attempts to break your spirit... sometimes from the inside out. And the survival story continues. And your inspiration shines. There are times when we forget about the reasons why we have come as far as we have. Who gives us the shoulders to stand on?

We should sit by your feet, eager to hear your "crick, crack" alerts, telling us you're ready to spread your enlightening tales. Instead, we are led astray by misleading characterizations of your people, and we mistake these false narratives for truth. It is not your truth. And even under the crumbling buildings, your spirit rises to the sky. No tremors can shake the foundation of your legacy. If the outsiders never again use a positive word for your people, it will not matter as long as you do not allow them to return your wrists and feet to chains. Eventually, time will heal this new wound, and the rest of the world may forget the pain and screams. But the memories should not be wiped from your mind and the desire to rebuild should not escape your dreams. You are the people of Toussaint L'Ouverture! Fight off the invaders, rebuild your nation and be your greatest hope of freedom!

Poet-economics

It's a mystery how we conceive mentally
And imprison ourselves with ignorant proclivities
I'm hanging by the thread of a dream
It ain't all what it seems
In my eye, I have the gleam
And I mean...
I'm fully evolved from the madness
The fads
The bags
The skinny jean's back mess
Not afraid to make my way in a big town
My style, my mind, and how I get around
Not a clown
But I smile right through it
Know quite a bit
Try to keep fit
But sometimes I slip into a false sense of security
And it's so immense when we believe in the Lynch fallacies
We start taking a fall
Sitting right here, just seeing it all...
From the view of my third floor window
Heard the sound of the gunshots like a great big crescendo
From the gutter, but I'm still here
The creed says to rise, all without fear...
Of failure
But there're several more layers
Glass ceiling barriers
Big wigs biting like terriers
But I remain, the introspective individual
"Esquire," the suffix, it must be a miracle
Because you never thought I'd make it this far
A member of the bar
Not the prison warden's star
And I'm still ready for the rebellion of Metropolis
Sons of Confederates' shook by the scale of Poet-economics.
Here comes the original, don't call me a copy
How far back are we going, calling a Black man a Nazi?

The Bushes
The "birthers"
The Glenn Beck worshippers
So many zombies; Limbaugh posers
Staged protests with ignorance in focus
Lies, distortion, scared the "coloreds" already got too much
Internal hatred
Nothing ever sacred
The King's passed and gone, so who're you gonna blame next?
Shamed of your reflection
Where's the love insurrection?
Everything the majority does doesn't equal perfection
Here's the first lesson of war and peace:
When the bombs are over Baghdad, all other concerns must cease
Sorry ma'am
We won't pay for this mammogram
Our funds gotta go to fightin' war in Afghanistan
And if we act now, Iran and Pakistan
Maybe we'll even have 4 or 5 more Viet-Nams
Your hold on the system is soft and fleeting
Knowledge of your deception can't stop breeding
Not distracted by your elementary games
New members in the crew, but you still sound the same
Got your hand on the trigger, but we all know the process
Your superiority – a myth, like the creature of Loch Ness
I keep the plan close to the vest
It sure isn't a guess of who you want left
Under attack if you're a brown or a black
Dragged from a truck or shot in the back
Police executions the day before your wedding
Supremacist militias deciding who we gon' let in
And I'm betting... the truth is where we last placed it
Over the mountaintop, caught up in the matrix.
Hope to get there with you in body and purpose
Wrapped in the rapture with spirited verses
The voices
The motions and the incense devotions
Never heard prose ever so potent
But if it's broken and we don't even know it
That you have to sound a certain way to be considered a poet
If YOUR tone DOES not FLOW LIKE THIS

You can't get a soul clap, you can't be legit
How did this happen? What could be the meaning?
Art isn't about rules, it's about feeling
Rebelling... against the will of the norm
My mind as the wind, my pen as the storm
I've got the remedy to get your spirit reborn
Pain without cries, love without scorn
Burning flags and bridges with something so toxic
Matriculate your studies in Poet-economics.

The Last Poem

This is the last poem that I have written tonight. But not the last poem I will ever write. But if this is THE last poem, let it be the first poem that shows you that a *poem can kill* old thoughts and *give life* to new dreams at the same time. Because the last poem should be more than some words on a page; let it be a revolution in a flourish of similes, sprinkled through rebellious stanzas. But this will be the last poem that allocates time for one of my own to say that we cannot do anything without the permission of someone else. Because I am tired of being told about being allowed to be a part of the process... allowed to protest... allowed to progress... allowed to have and fulfill the promise. And with this last poem we will take our freedom by poetic bullet and ballot. Thus, the last poem should be bold and courageous, strong and dangerous. And this poem will not petition or be in competition to be given a token position at the left corner of the *"white has to be right"* round table. Because the last poem will ask, "if not now, when?" When?! Because it is 2010, and the last poem cannot try to be patient for another 400 years to be *given* freedom... to be given rights... to be given privileges... to be given power... And 40 years after the deaths of Malcolm and Martin, the last poem cannot be afraid to be in power. If not here, then where? Here, on this land built on the sweat, tears, blood and backs of our ancestors dreaming and holding on to long ago memories of freedom. Not why, but why not? Because if we must exist here, in this time, at this moment in history, in this world, then why not be liberated enough to have faith in our own greatness and majesty. So, if this is the last poem you hear or read tonight, I hope it is the first poem that makes you believe.